The Compass to Self-Healing - The Self-Help Book

How to consciously follow your inner voice to awaken your primal trust step by step and heal your inner child

Marlene Nanninga

CONTENT

What you can expect in this book

You read the word "self-healing" and you are skeptical and a bit curious? Your mind says "No," but your gut is saying "Yes, you are!" It's a little inner struggle to find the primal trust that we all lost a little and more and more somewhere in our childhood in the system we grew up in.

URVERTRAUEN! Let this word melt on your tongue. To dare to do something, to trust in our primordial being. A subcategory of primordial confidence is self-confidence. The feeling of being able to cope with life and its demands. So we have the feeling of being able to cope with any situation, any new challenge, and find a way to deal with it. So it's a basic feeling. Have you ever wondered why some things in this world feel so wrong, and questioned, "Does it have to be this way?", I'm going to say flat out, "No." After all, it doesn't have to be anything and only you know exactly what is good for you. *You don't know at the moment? Well then, welcome to your new path to yourself. In this book, I'll give you thoughts, ideas, and exercises piece by piece that you can implement for yourself in the way that feels right for you. At your pace, with your color, with your taste.* Just as and who you are, and if you want to reinvent yourself, - do it! Now is the right time to do it.

In this book you can expect an attempt at regression, remembrance, reminding our, your primordial self-trust: one of the foundations for a functioning self-healing. I offer you methods, techniques, mind games and you use them how and when you want. I give a framework, you paint it. Just as you like. Are you motivated? Do you want to find a new way back to yourself?

Back to inner confidence, calm and wisdom?

Well, go ahead, I look forward to seeing you!

> "THE POWER THAT CREATED THE BODY IS
> ALSO ABLE TO HEAL THE BODY".
> HEAL."
> (DR. JOE DISPENZA)

The terms

PRIMAL TRUST & SELF CONFI-DENCE

"That inner emotional security that a child develops in the first months of life." (psychological definition)
Basic trust is a stable, social attitude. Self-confidence, on the other hand, is a stable attitude toward one's own abilities.

The child thus develops the positive basic feeling that it can trust people and itself, that they are well-meaning and reliable. The basic trust thus essentially arises from the positive experience, which corresponds between the world and the personal need.

In addition, the primal mistrust should be mentioned, which naturally arises when a child experiences the opposite, i.e. no reliability, perhaps even violence.

Courage or shyness, the ability to get involved in relationships and to allow closeness depend on the extent of the acquired basic trust. So, now I am writing about other persons with whom the individual can make contact and allow closeness, if he has a healthy basic trust. But is primordial trust to be equated with basic trust and a good bond with oneself? In the time when a child develops a good basic trust, he should also have developed a good self-confidence. With a good constitution of the social foundation, when needs are met at the right time with sufficient love, the growing child gets a positive self-perception. Now many things happen in the course of life and some events make this basic confidence shake. Then it is important to work on allowing this basic feeling to find its way back into our lives.

So, when we discover in adolescence or even adulthood that we lack basic trust, we should first allow closeness to ourselves and want to get to know ourselves before we allow ourselves to be seduced by the desires and needs of others. So we should arrive at ourselves first, before we can decide where and how it then goes on for us.

Isn't that actually what we find so incredibly difficult in adulthood? We work, we do, we function well, but something is not right. And that 'something' is the connection to self. The self is talking to you. Mostly very quietly. Loud, on the other hand, is usually the ego (little secret tip). It would be hilarious if you lived in a temple with others who don't communicate with you. And our body sometimes thinks it is the spirit. But it isn't. We have 3 pillars that are old familiar to us: Body, Mind and Spirit.

> *"How can you heal yourself if you don't know who you are?" (Kathleen Koch)*

SELF-HEALING

Where does it start, where does it end? What is actually true about self-healing? Is there really such a thing?

> Can I just always heal myself, no matter how I eat, how much I do, with an unhealthy lifestyle?
> Is it possible to flick your finger and just conjure everything up?

No, unfortunately not. But why unfortunately, it would be very boring if it were so simple. The path to yourself is a wonderful one, I say that from my own experience. It can be tingling and refreshing to rediscover yourself, if you are open to it and if the focus is on the positive.

That is exactly where self-healing begins. It needs a healthy basis, a conscious handling of oneself and the right and loving thought for oneself. If you have chosen an unhealthy way of life and want to continue it, then just put this book away. It will not help you. You may try one thing or another, but you will say it doesn't work, and you will advertise the possibility of self-healing to others because of your bad experience, thus negatively affecting others. *Self-healing is a choice.* And this is not hocus-pocus, it has always had a deeper meaning. Our western medicine also understands more and more that there is more than pain pills and symptom treatment and that was already aware of many healers in ancient times.

Self-healing is a choice.
Choose to live a life that is healthy for you, and pay attention to the small signs of everyday life,

because they can show you very clearly what is unhealthy for you.

> Consequently, a few questions that you should answer as honestly and accurately as possible:
>
> - How much time do you invest in your job?
> - How much time do you invest in your family?
> - How much time do you invest in a harmonious family life?
> - How much time do you invest in your household?
> - How much time do you invest in making your house, apartment or property look the way others would like it?
> - How much time do you invest in your weekly shopping?
> - How much time do you spend buying things you don't need?
> - How much time do you invest looking at things you don't need?
> - How much time do you invest to prepare a healthy meal?
> - How much time do you invest to have a good and close conversation with your partner?
> - And when do you have time for yourself?

What in your life is mischief that your self wants to be healed?

What are you currently doing? What are you trying to build up and break down in your current phase of life?

• What important desires/issues or talents to develop would you like to focus more on in your journey?

• What could you do to be more in tune with your strengths and abilities in your life?

• What mark do you want to leave behind when your life comes to an end?

• If you never had to work, what would you do instead?

• If you didn't have to watch money in any way, what would you do?

• Which of your dreams have been waiting a long time to be realized?

• What motivates you?

• Name things you are proud of.

• Name people and things that inspire you.

• If you had more courage, what would you do?

• What would you like to spend more time doing?

• What things calm you down?

• What is important to you in a relationship?

• When you have a pain, where exactly is the pain located?

• Which organ is behind it? Which subject could it be? E.G.: Stomach = stomach ulcer = being sour + not being able to speak your mind/feeling at the mercy of others.

Phew, a lot of questions, you're thinking to yourself now, aren't you? Sometimes an answer is difficult, sometimes an answer comes easily, and that, I can tell you, is perfectly fine. Self-healing, as you can already imagine, is an inner process. This process needs patience, trust, dedication and gratitude.

In the following I entrust you with a true story from my life and perhaps it will encourage you to continue on this path step by step and face the mistrust that has probably grown a lot with your lifetime.

Being skeptical of others is perfectly healthy. Not every person we meet is honest with us. Check mindfully and listen, but don't lose confidence in yourself. Just because someone else may not have treated you the way that would have been good for you, you don't have to punish yourself all your life by not trusting yourself now. So rebuild a good foundation with yourself. It has helped me a lot. Now my personal story for you.

What you have always suspected: It works.

AND SUDDENLY HE WAS THERE AGAIN: MY STOMACH GATE-KEEPER (A TRUE STORY)

As a child, I suffered from severe stomach pain to stomach cramps, so severe that even the emergency doctor had to come now and then to give me an injection: I had a stomach ulcer. And this stomach ulcer remained for many years, then it was called chronic gastritis and they said I had to live with it. This chronic gastritis meant that at some point I no longer had a stomach gate and every time I moved down, upside down, I would get this stomach acid washed into my mouth. It was horrible. It was miserable, it was really absolutely not nice anymore. And I was young and I didn't feel like living with it at all, because I loved doing uneven bars. But ... I wasn't a kid anymore, and I wasn't exposed to what I had to swallow as a kid. That resentment I had to swallow every day, that injustice, that intrigue, that stupid feeling of being at the mercy of it and not being able to do anything. It's better to shut up, I thought to myself as a child, because I had to make the experience that if you don't shut up, you don't get applause for it, you get a beating. It was terrible and at some point I was 19 and understood: I'm still alive, I have everything in my hands now! So I decided to carry out an experiment on myself. I framed this experiment in time and gave it a full year. My goal: MY MAGEN PROMOTER!

I became involved with higher-level issues at an early age. I started to be interested in other religions when I was 11. I was baptized Catholic. I learned about yoga and meditations and became involved with cancer and why cancer comes and how it goes. I bought a book by Louise L. Hay on affirmations. Of course, affirmations don't work unless you change your situation, situation and life to the point where it is healthy for you. Just telling yourself that everything is fine when nothing is fine doesn't work. This should be clear to all of us. So it is important to look awake at why we react to something and why a disease has overtaken us.

OUR BODY ALWAYS WANTS TO TALK TO US! Always be aware of this.

It sets signs. Moles appear, there is a regular tugging somewhere, you notice something again and again - LISTEN TO IT! It would be lunatic, if we would live in a living temple, which would NOT communicate with us. Or?

So I decided to listen to my body, to listen into it. I bought a book about organs, about the structure of our body and felt back into it and started creating little *light meditations.* At first, I generally imagined bright (healing) light flowing through my body. I imagined healing light as a kind of waterfall, flowing through me from the top of my head all the way down to my feet, washing all the weight I was carrying into the ground with it. So I lightened up and it was a sacred healing inner process of my self and it brought me back to myself. So I went ahead and lay down 2 times a day and very concretely imagined my stomach gate starting to wake up again. This I did for a whole year. And I felt better and better, lighter and lighter, less and less acid bubbled up my throat and suddenly I could bend over without that acid wetting my mouth.

So I went back to the doctor and had a gastroscopy done and there it was again: my stomach gate!

So I was able to experience it myself on the basis of my stomach gatekeeper more than 15 years ago and since then I have experienced many beautiful little miracles. Of course, there are many doubters, many envious people and people who do not grant you a cure, simply also for the reason that you may then no longer have much desire to spend your valuable time with people who talk you out of the beautiful life.

Realize: this decision will change your life. Once you could realize that with love and patience and visualization many things are possible, your horizon will be broadened in the long run and you will no longer look to the plate, you will look over it. Or perhaps you will no longer need a plate at all. What would that be like? How does that feel? Incredible? Incredibly good? Light? Again, pay attention to your body awareness. Is something fidgeting? Is something rejoicing? Is something excited? Is something afraid?

All feelings and emotions are allowed to be. This is important. Just accept it, as I have accepted it, and become an explorer of yourself. Look with curiosity at what is happening inside you. Let it tingle between you and be your best friend, because body, mind and spirit share a home, it is beneficial to be the best friend of that place. Let's just call this place: temple. Or do you have another beautiful idea? Write it down!

Why am I telling you my personal story? Because I can and because I want you to be able to as well. Believe in yourself, get closer to yourself again and be your best friend. Do what you have always wanted to do. Do good to yourself. Think good thoughts, be kind to your body and take care of yourself. I hereby invite you to go on a journey to find yourself. And do you know what I have understood through this experience? I understood that self-efficacy is a really important part of who we are. When we ourselves have the belief that we are competent enough to successfully perform a desired action by ourselves, it creates new paths and worlds.

As we all know, faith moves mountains. Doesn't it?

> "If I am capable of my spirit, I am also capable of healing myself." Dieter Broers

Welcome to your journey to SELF. I am glad that you have chosen this journey.

You have turned off your cell phone, decided to just be for yourself and question yourself? You can't be bothered right now because you've done everything you can to create a protected space for yourself? Not yet? Do it now!

Create an hour of space for yourself in your everyday life again and again, preferably in the morning or/and in the evening. Or travel with yourself to another place for a weekend, every now and then, to be allowed to be with yourself and be who you are until you find out who you are. You don't know who you are yet? You will find out step by step, on your journey to yourself.

You are safe and protected.
You have everything you need right now.
You only get tasks that you can actually solve.

Be sure you have the opportunity you need and do yourself the favor of manipulating yourself less.

Your body will occasionally knock on this journey and make you feel old cravings. This is normal because your body has been emotionally

and chemically conditioned for many years to fall
back into old familiar stimuli and patterns. It's a
kind of safety. So treat yourself with care, as you
would a newborn child. Your body wants to cling
to the past and you give it the safe ground and loving encouragement that it is fine the way it is and
this journey will be a beautiful and healing one. It
will feel sore and that's okay, it's a very sensitive
process that you have chosen and you will be very
grateful for it at the latest at the end of life when
you can say: I did the best I could to live the way
it felt right for me, because "Death is not pre-
vented by fear, but life is", and why most people
chose a path away from themselves: because of
fear. The fear of not being accepted, the fear of being ostracized, the fear of doing something wrong,
the fear of being wrong.

But you have never been wrong, as a primordial essence you knew your soul plan and that is
where you want to go back to. Self-healing also
has something to do with your individual soul
plan and healing of the self does not mean that
you now compulsively want to change something
pathological in the shortest possible time, or even
suppress or banish it. **Self-healing means to**

create order within yourself again. And how do you do that? By taking yourself by the hand, talking to yourself lovingly and asking yourself: Who am I? And where do I want to go? Who was I once and what did I think I wanted to do and be here on earth?

Become aware that life in general always means change.

"The best way to take care of the future is to turn carefully to the present," Thich Nhat Hanh once said, and he wasn't wrong. It is your daily decision that you make, what you do, where you go, what you occupy yourself with, what you burden yourself with, what you accept as a task and what you do not.

And for this, there are methods you can use to find yourself again a little bit.

I provide you with questions, should you not be able to answer them right away, ask your soul and ask: What would my soul like to write there? Or: What would I have written if I were still a child? Or: If I didn't have to do all the things I always have to do, what would I most like to do? Try to get in touch with yourself with calmness and gentleness and trick your ego a little. The ego will probably tell you a time or two that what you are doing is total nonsense. Don't reject your ego, that only makes your ego bigger, accept it, thank it for that message and just move on. Be good to yourself, make yourself some tea, take good care of yourself and move on.

Learn to differentiate

What am I?

What is adapted?

What are things and behaviors, patterns that I have developed to meet needs of others?

What am I doing for others: for loved ones/for my immediate private environment/for my work environment and what am I doing for myself?

What of all this feels good and what doesn't?

Pay attention to your heart.

How does it feel? Is it easy or hard when you ask yourself questions? With every little word, pay attention to how your heart behaves. It is talking to you.

The same applies to your belly. Get to know and accept your body and its language again. Feel free to say to yourself, "Listen to yourself!" You don't have to go too far if it doesn't feel good to you. But sometimes your gut goes in circles when there's an issue that may be looked at. Reassure yourself that you will take good care of yourself and stop doing things that don't feel good. It will be a little strange at first if those around you are not used to such behavior from you. And you don't have to explain yourself, you can just say, "It doesn't feel right to me."

There can be no healing if you do not listen to your own body.

Where are your roots?

What can you connect to?

Differentiate and make conscious choices:

Do you notice that you have something to nibble on that is affecting your physical ailments?

Then ask yourself the following questions and make yourself aware:

• Is it my wound?

• Or is it a wound of my ancestors/lineage/from my ancestral field?

• Or is it entirely a wound of someone in my immediate circle?

FRIENDS PACKAGE

We humans are originally very sensitive beings and also get vibrations of our environment and therefore it is also possible that you have noticed and accepted something that is not yours at all. If you want, you can confidently return this with the following visualization:

I suggest you take an undisturbed walk in nature. Connect with the trees, the little plants, the birds and insects. Say hello to them, even if it may seem a little silly to you at first. You are a part of this earth and your environment and everything belongs together. The animals, the plants, the trees say hello, so say hello back. Be kind to your environment. Notice the plants consciously: which ones are the ones that appeal to you the most? And just walk and get into a good walking feeling. To do this, please don't just walk 5 steps and then return to your car because the wind is blowing or because it's starting to drizzle; can you think of any other excuse? Neither the wind nor the rain will kill you.

You might even go so far as to feel real life again, because our everyday social life often doesn't allow that anymore. So you are on the road and you have consciously arrived where you are. You smell the plants around you, you breathe deeply, you perceive, and you might just feel like you're in a little sweet grape or cloud. That's perfectly fine.

Now, during your walk, feel inside yourself how much you are carrying mentally? Are you carrying only your mental backpack or are you perhaps also carrying the mental backpack of your mother or your friend? If you notice that you are not only carrying your backpack, you can, if you like, make a very clear decision: Stop, visualize this person whose mental backpack you seem to be carrying in addition, and give the backpack back to this person with the following words, **"I noticed that I am carrying your backpack, and I am giving it back to you. Here you go!"**, actually perform a hand gesture that returns a backpack, and do so with a clear decision, that is, also with the intention that you really will not continue to carry this backpack.

You can also tell this visualized person why you are no longer doing this. It is possible for you to also tell this person, **"I feel your pain, I feel with you. I choose not to suffer with you and leave your pain with you and give it back to you,"** or **"I feel you. I feel for you. I leave you your choice to suffer. I make myself free of your suffering. I keep what is mine and give back what is yours."**

But be careful: Don't permanently go into the victim role. Stand up, don't make yourself small, but tall and straight. You do not have to stand above the other person, you are now at eye level. Perhaps there is also anger in you. Then finally let the anger out! Maybe you also want to scold and denounce the other person that it is unfair that you have carried this backpack for so long, so long

that you hardly noticed that it is not your backpack anymore.

Energetically, it is healthy to let out everything of emotions first in a protected space (which
is nature) and framework (you should not get into
this for days, but make a clear decision and have
that clarified and relieved in one hour), and then
at the end return to the upright and steadfast pos-
ture and say: **"I am going into my own responsibility. I'm carrying my backpack now, just
my backpack. I'm sure you can manage to
carry your own backpack, too, and if not, it's
not my responsibility to take it off your
hands permanently."**

If you always take over things for others, it is
not possible for the others to come into personal
responsibility at all. They will always be sublimi-
nally dependent on you or others. Be kind enough
to let these people decide for themselves for their
lives, even though you may not like the decision.
It is not your life, it is their life, and they have the
right to decide and stand up for their lives. Just as
you have that right.

If the backpack is from your ancestral lineage, you can decide whether you work up this topic for your ancestral lineage or not. Consciously accept this issue or consciously release it! **"I feel the burden of XY. I choose to face/not face this issue and resolve/not resolve/pass on/accept those in this life of mine."**

If you should have taken care of this wound, it is now your wound: great!

Now ask yourself; How, where and when do you feel this wound? What issue could possibly be behind it? Where do you feel a twinge and pinch or discomfort? In what part of your body? Which organ?

The inner voice

In each of us there is an inner voice that can tell us how we really feel. If this voice is suppressed or you are used to not paying attention to it, it may be very thin, perhaps squeaky, but it exists. And the more you listen to it and listen to it, the stronger and clearer that voice will become.

Intuition - that funny feeling - tells you when you are in danger on the road. It makes you switch to the other side of the road or run a detour. It is your sixth sense.

Every person experiences their inner voice differently. Maybe you have bad dreams or a headache, maybe you feel exhausted. You suddenly stuff an immense amount of chips into yourself or you realize you have cleaned the apartment several times within two days. **What is important is not what you experience, but that you see it as a message.**

When you open up to your feelings, you cannot choose among them: They belong together! **Each of us needs feelings.**

It is on the basis of feelings that we develop our insights and the ability to orient ourselves and make the right decisions. Feelings, even painful feelings, are allies that let us know what is going on inside us and often how we should react to situations.

In order to make contact with your body, you must live in your body and pay attention to the sensations that arise. Sensations that you perceive in your body are just that: feelings.

Fear tightens your throat, you tremble, your stomach tightens, it takes your breath away. Tears well up, your lap becomes wet, your hands tingle.

If you have ignored your body for a long time, it probably seems strange to adjust to these perceptions.

Or you can feel these processes in your body, you may describe uninvolved, but you do not know what they mean.

Young children can't say "I'm scared." they say "My tummy feels funny." when adults give this perception a name, the child learns to associate the sensation with the feeling.

If no one has paid attention to your feelings and you have never learned to name your sensations, you will start all over again and learn by yourself to understand these messages that your body is giving you.

The better you can accept your feelings without judging them, the easier it will be for you to experience them, work with them, and learn from them.

If you are used to hiding your feelings, it may happen so quickly and involuntarily that you don't even have a chance to feel the original feeling. You start to feel happy and slip into restlessness. You feel angry and immediately you hate yourself. *Each of us humans has different patterns.*

The more you feel, the easier it becomes. Your fear of your feelings will become smaller and smaller. You will be less able to push your sensations aside, and it will hurt a bit or two, but you will feel relieved. Feelings are independent and have value in themselves, but if you are familiar with them, a feeling that you do not associate with a specific event might cause you anxiety.

EMOTIONAL EXERCISE

What are feelings?

Say the following list clearly and each word several times, with different tones of voice and intonation, louder or softer. Pay attention to your feelings as you say each word.

What sensations does the word awaken in you? How does your body feel? Do some words suit you and others not? Write down any other words that specifically describe you. When you are finished, underline the three words that you respond to most strongly:

- enthusiastic
- tenderly
- sad
- hilarious

- lonely
- irritable
- disappointed
- fearful
- satisfied
- happy
- depressed
- shy
- violated
- jealous
- affectionate
- ...

People often confuse feelings with thoughts or observations.

"I don't feel like that was fair."

"I have a feeling you're going to leave me."

These are statements about your thoughts, not your feelings. To find out if a statement is about thoughts, you can use "I believe" instead of "I have a feeling." If it makes sense, it is more likely to be a thought or an observation.

"I feel hurt by what you did."

"I'm afraid you might leave me."

You notice the difference?

If you are in contact with people who respect your feelings and who are also well connected to their own feelings, you can accelerate this learning process. Through their feedback, their example, their gentleness, you can learn to connect with your own feelings.

SHOW YOUR FEELINGS AND TELL YOUR FACE.

There is no one right way to show emotions. Each of us has our own style. But it's important that you're able to express what you're feeling in a way that feels right to you and that your facial expression matches how you're feeling.

LEARN RESPECTFUL EXPRESSION OF YOUR FEELINGS

"I'm pissed. When you're late and don't call, I get worried. Please call me next time." instead of "You are the most inconsiderate person I know. You don't care about my feelings at all."

If you have something to say that is important to you or where you will be exposed and vulnerable, don't undermine your position by picking an awkward moment when you are unlikely to meet an attentive ear. You should give yourself, your friends, your partner, your child or children a fair starting position.

DISTINGUISH

Come to a balanced decision about when it is appropriate to express your feelings. Not every relationship is a close one. So weigh when it is appropriate and when it is not.

LEARN TO SHOW YOUR ANGER WITHOUT VIOLENCE

Anger is a feeling, violence is a behavior.

Many people don't know they are angry until that anger explodes. Learning to notice the signs of your anger will help you manage your violence.

How do you act when you are upset?

- Do you get mean? Do you blame others?
- Do you behave in a particularly nice way?
- Are you starting to laugh?
- Are you withdrawing?
- Do you fail to keep appointments?
- Or are you too late?
- Can you not eat or sleep then?
- Or do you sleep more than usual?

"I feel anger rising inside me. I need some time to myself. I'll be back in an hour," in this way you communicate directly what is going on, you take responsibility for your feelings and you give yourself and others the secure feeling that you are determined to avoid violence. Just be with your feeling, go for a walk, give your feeling space and don't get any stupid thoughts, so don't go drinking anything alcoholic, don't transfigure your mind. Just stay with yourself and your feeling. Hold on to it. You can do it!

As arranged, you come back after an hour, not earlier, not later. This is how you build trust. Ask the person you were upset with if they would like to talk to you about it. If you both want to, talk to each other: what upset you? Why did you have to get out? If you have a hard time talking about it, just come back to it later.

YOU DESPAIR?

1. Take a breath. Breathe!
2. Count your breaths.
3. Breathe out longer than you breathe in.
4. Make yourself some tea.
5. Get a stuffed animal, pillow or blanket to snuggle with.
6. Put on a relaxation CD.
7. Call your best friend or pastoral care. (If you are well, make a list of people and their phone numbers who are well willing and will listen to you when you need it).
8. Pet your pet or your pillow.
9. Water the flowers.
10. Do yoga.
11. Take a hot bath.
12. Smell your favorite fragrance.
13. Write many times, "I am safe. I like myself. Others like me. I can relax now."

14. Jog.

15. Prayer.

16. Meditate.

17. Cry into your pillow what you have previously stroked.

18. Watch a funny movie or read a comedy.

19. Order your favorite food.

20. Go to the forest and listen to nature.

21. Go to the lake and put your feet in the water.

22. Draw circles in the sand.

23. Embrace.

24. And start again from the top, if you should need it.

You can make yourself a new list, but please always put breathing first.

Despair, self-loathing and panic are intense feelings, give yourself rest after this effort. Take good care of yourself. When you have come to rest, ask yourself:

• What's the last thing you remember before it hit you?

• Where were you and with whom?

• Has anything happened to you in the last two days that has bothered you?

• Did you suspect a different feeling before you lost your composure?

• And have you had this before?

• Do you have a lot of stress, time pressure or worries at the moment?

• Have you had to think about something that made you uncomfortable and quickly pushed it aside?

• Did you remember anything that made you uncomfortable?

• Body contact is important! Massage yourself, stroke your hand or put your hand on your shoulder. Be caring, a good mother or father to yourself. Be affectionate with yourself, just as you wanted to be when you were a child. Your childhood is not over!

• How are you?

• Yes, I'm sure you've noticed, it's a deep and wonderful process and that's a good thing.

When you open something that you have been hiding from you for a long time, it may stink and look disgusting at first. Like a cheese bread in a box that was unfortunately in the fridge for far too long. The difference with the cheese bread is that the cheese bread spoils no matter how long you look at it, but you heal when you look at yourself and take yourself seriously and accept and embrace and love yourself for who you are. You are allowed to love yourself for who you are. Even if you stink.

PARTNERSHIP, TRUST AND CLOSENESS

You may wonder what your self-healing has to do with your partnership, and I will tell you: a lot! If you find that you are so close with a person just because you live together and you may share your belongings and achievements and prestige, it does not mean for a long time that it is a functioning, loving and honest partnership.

For a self-healing process, the general framework is important.

You yourself cannot heal if you are constantly confronted with people who do not accept you as you are, or who do not respect you, or where a great many injuries have already occurred over time and the relationship of trust has been immensely damaged. In the following I will ask you a few questions and you will see from the answers to what extent your partnership has a fertile ground or not.

1. Do you respect your partner?

2. Does your partner respect you?

3. Can you talk openly with each other?

4. Do you handle conflict well?

5. Do you both compromise or just one?

6. Do give and take alternate?

7. Can you show your real feelings?

8. Can you talk to your partner about events that have been very stressful for you?

9. Is your partner open to exploring new avenues with you?

10. Does your partnership give you enough space for your personal development and for change?

11. Can you achieve your own goals within your relationship?

12. Does your partner support you in making changes that you consciously seek?

13. Is your partner willing to help you?

If you were able to answer yes to most of the questions, it is probably a stable and functioning relationship. If you weren't sure of the answers, the relationship may still be very fresh or you may not be asking enough of the relationship to know what to expect and what not to expect. If you had to answer no most of the time, you should seriously consider changing or ending this relationship.

You deserve a good relationship!
You may think you have no influence at all on who you enter into a relationship with. As your self-esteem grows, it will seem normal to you that other people like or love you. You will realize that you can say no to some people and consciously choose others.

In new relationships, try to consciously practice trust and closeness. Relationships can be rewarding even if you are short and do not give you everything.

As a framework in which you can learn understanding, trust, and friendly give and take, such relationships provide a healthy foundation for inner growth.

Sexual healing requires a certain base of trust and goodwill between you and your lover. If you have found a sensitive, understanding person, that is wonderful. If not, you are not alone in this, many feel this way. Don't give up and settle for someone who is not good for you just so you won't be alone.

Learn well to be alone with yourself.

You are worth it to yourself. You deserve loving support in your healing.

Lead healthy relationships

Imagine two loving people who are aware of projections and perceptual irritations and want to find a way to deal with them. This brings with it a high potential.

The illusion of security is one of the main reasons why we need relationships in the first place. In a healing relationship, illusion has no more room, because illusion always leads to disappointment in the end. Loyalty, friendship and reliability, on the other hand, provide a healthy framework for a healthy relationship; possessiveness and need for control and mutual sabotage do not.

Healing can only happen in a space where we experience freedom, where we are allowed to be authentically who we are.

So what do I mean by freedom here? I don't mean free love, I don't mean being able to jump into bed with everyone and everything. I mean letting the other person be the way he or she is, without exerting control. To give him or her the space to develop, to let him or her blossom. To be aware of this and in joy, the decision to have chosen each other, to be allowed to walk this path together and to meet again and again.

Such a relationship requires both partners to be aware of possible projections and to constantly question them.

A healthy humility, so to speak.

My point is this:
Take a look at yourself first, especially when it hurts the most, before blaming your partner for anything that may not be.

And if you get into projections, hold each other.

No one is free of projections, it's how we deal with them that's important. And so it's important to recognize that and to support each other in that and to grow together. Yes, this requires great integrity and sensitivity, because most of the time projections are fraught with many emotions.

You may learn to admit when you are projecting and practice closeness with your partner instead of demanding control, ownership and dependence.

Compassion and unconditional trust and total respect are prerequisites for this. Nobody is more right, nobody is more to blame, nobody is weaker or stronger. Stay at eye level with your partner.

Such a relationship may demand a lifetime of jumping over one's own shadow, of opening one's space and heart again and again, even when our emotions threaten to overwhelm us.
In our society we have learned early on that showing pain and weakness seems to be a form of losing recognition.

Let's lift this misconception.

Just the showing of weakness and pain is a strength in itself. There is no longer a mask that has to pretend. You can really show yourself as you are and go along with a person as long as your journey together lasts. Because you can be so open, vulnerable and touched, you will see the field of trust it reveals. It is beautiful!

The work with the inner child

"I felt like all my successes were just one big scam because I ignored the little kid who never dealt with it and still lives a life of humiliation and pain because of it."

You hate a part of yourself when you hate the child within you. Without that part in you, you have no access to its gentleness, yieldingness, its ability to trust and wonder.

When you open yourself to taking care of your inner child, you will learn to lovingly accept yourself.

Even if it feels ambivalent at first, accepting this part of yourself is an important part of your healing.

Start listening to your inner child, listening to that little voice and respecting it and bringing it joy. Be the loving parent of your inner child.

WRITING EXERCISE: THE CHILD IN YOU

Here you can get in touch with the child within you. If you are able to love and comfort the little child within you, if you can allow your adult self to express the compassion you feel for that little child, then write it now and tell him or her. You can address this letter directly to him or her, or you can enter into a letter dialogue with him or her by first writing as an adult and then responding as a child.

If you do not yet feel any emotion, tenderness or connection with the child, first write how you honestly feel. You can't write, "I love you. I will take care of you," if that is a lie. Start with, "I'm willing to sit down and write to you, even though I'm not entirely sure you exist," or "I don't even like you yet," or even "I hate you, you got me into this shit in the first place." Every point of connection is a beginning. You can't have a loving relationship if you don't make contact first. Take the first step.

If you can't do anything with the child inside you, imagine another child who was the same age as you were when you had to disconnect from yourself. Try writing to this one instead. This is a good exercise to do more often, especially if you don't feel compassion at first. Eventually you will be able to tell the little child that he is innocent and that you will protect him.

HELPER

The ultimate in self-healing is an immune system that you yourself are in good contact with. So always work to make sure that it is stable. If it is not, deal with yourself and work to get it back to stability. Sounds simple, it is, as long as you follow certain rules. In the following I will provide you with a few little helpers that you can use and apply or that you can rearrange in a way that suits you.

Find your way back to a faith
To believe in yourself and that this life means well for you.

Create focus on the positive in your life and continually work on things you want to see in your life that are good for you.
Self-healing can only happen if you fundamentally take good care of yourself.

Here I'll give you a few ideas:

Morning ritual
You have already prepared the start for the morning in the evening. You have already put quiet music in the player so that you do not have to search in the morning. You are now the proud owner of an incense burner and you have one or more good smelling incense blends and charcoal tablets that you choose in the morning depending on your mood. Smell the mixture and you will know which one is up for smoking today. Light the incense and smoke out your room for a few minutes, then open the window wide and you turn on some quiet music. Meanwhile, quietly prepare your morning drink and then give yourself fifteen minutes of

complete rest. Arrive at that wonderful morning. Sit quietly back in your bed or on a pillow. Get comfortable and just notice. You are now allowed to just be. Allow your thoughts to flow. Allow yourself to think, but don't give the thoughts an answer. And also be aware in everyday life that not every thought you think is worth paying attention to. Only perceive.

> - What do you smell?
> - What do you feel?
> - What do you think?
> - Smile!
> - Now consciously come into gratitude.
> - Say to yourself: **Thank you for allowing me to consciously experience this day.**
> - **Thank you for giving me wonderful challenges.**
> - Thank you for giving me such a wonderful temple.
> - I am taken care of. I am safe and in the here and now.

Enjoy with aromatherapy

When we perceive fragrant flowers, we often hold our nose to the blossom to inhale its fragrance deeply. This shows that we humans love fragrant plants.

We forget our daily worries and needs in this moment and everything seems carefree at once. Plants produce these fragrances, store them in their tissues and when touched or warmed, they release them. Of all the plants that exist on earth, only about one percent produce essential oils. People since ancient times particularly appreciate these plants, which can be used to make perfumes, fragrances and medicine.

Aromatherapy uses the healing, gentle effect on the body and mind that essential oils possess. The oils promote relaxation, increase well-being and can be applied to the skin (with a carrier oil), used as a bath additive or inhaled. Completely pure essential oils, as in the link, can even be ingested.

Personally, good smells help me a lot. So I decided to use high quality and pure essential oils for myself. Maybe this will help you too.

Be curious like a little child what sees new.

A drop of peppermint oil to a liter of water promotes the elimination of toxins that are in us. One of the top helpers.

Consequently, I put together a table of useful helpers for you. You are welcome to expand this for yourself.

Purifying effect of herbs, spices, woods and fruits

Plant	supports	cleans from
Incense	Calming, meditation	Aggression, tension
Myrrh	Inspiration	Lack of imagination
Sandalwood	Calming, sensuality	Anxiety, stress, tension
Juniper	Protection, stimulation	Anxiety, dullness
Spruce needles	Refreshment	dammed up energy
Eucalyptus	Healing	Illness, colds
Cinnamon	Healing, sensuality	Illness, unkindness
Cedar wood	Relaxation	Stress, tension
Sage	positive energy	all imbalances
Rosemary	Friendship, concentration	Discord, learning problems
Thyme	Strength, activity	Weakness, despondency

Lavender	Relaxation, intuition	Tensions, nightmares
Chamomile	Healing, harmony	Illness, dispute
Peppermint	Healing, freshness	Illness, dull energy
Angelica	Protection	Ghosts
Catnip	Animal love	Unkindness
Citrus	Refreshment, concentration	Learning problems, fatigue
Apple	Love, fertility	Unkindness, loneliness
Rose	Love, relaxation	Unkindness, stress
Cloves	Power, protection	Lack of drive, anxiety
Hyacinth	Healing	Heartbreak
Verbena	Protection	Nightmares

> "The best medicine is to teach people how not to need one". Hippocrates

CREATE A TARGET COLLAGE FOR YOURSELF

Imagining and visualizing your goals is already the first step. With a goal collage you help yourself to keep your focus and align yourself.

You keep your goals, dreams and desires in mind and thus create a new path in life already in your mind.

To do this, collect images, beliefs and key-words around your own goal that will help and motivate you to achieve it.

Now stick your collection on a DIN-A3 or DIN-A2 sized cardboard and hang it up visible to you.

Cut out pictures of a magazine that look like freedom and liveliness. People who hike and look happy. People who look healthy and content in their old age. Places you wish you could be some-day. Activities you'd like to do, such as meditating yogis. Pictures of recipes that are healthy and delicious.

Write **diary** regularly, every evening, every two days or every week:

Integrate your small collage of goals into your diary. You'll be amazed at what you've accomplished after a year when you look back at your diary from the beginning. Your diary helps you to keep focus. Write down things you want to change and things you find beautiful.

And if you ever want to blow off steam, do that too.

Write on a loose piece of paper to a fictitious person you have chosen to help you. Write down your frustration and burden and burn that piece of paper with the words, **"It's all gone now!"**

QUIET SAFE PLACE

Create a quiet, safe place in your home:

Use a corner in your room and create a small altar for yourself. You can hang your target collage above this altar and place a small cabinet in front of it, on which your incense burner stands, which you now use every morning for your morning ritual. A candle next to the teapot creates even more coziness. Also, a candle eats bad smells and makes LIGHT.

LIGHT MEDITATIONS

Sit with a pillow in front of your newly developed, small, quiet and safe place. Turn off your phone, put it on airplane mode or silent. Allow yourself to be undisturbed for 15 minutes.

Worries, fears and emotions look worse in the dark than in the light.

In order to make healthy choices for yourself and your life, it's important to shine a light on the darkness. *Light the candle:*

Now calmly breathe deeply in and out and repeat this more times until you notice that you are calming down. With each breath, blow out negative thoughts and emotions, feelings and breathe in lightness. Pay attention to the light of the candle and visually absorb this light. Close your eyes and now focus on your light within you. There is a small ball of light in your belly, with each breath this ball of light gets bigger and bigger and your feeling in your belly gets wider and lighter. Feel how this ball of light grows until you yourself are sitting in this ball of light. The brighter your inner space becomes, the more your fears and worries disappear. You are light. You are your own

healing. You have absolute power over yourself. You are pure. Pure light. Questions may arise within you. Ask these questions in your sacred light space and listen for answers. Be patient, the answer will come. If you do not hear an answer, then be sure, your answer is already in your heart. You have been heard and you are provided for. Feel the warmth that surrounds you and enjoy. Enjoy this moment of perfection in being. You are perfect. You are completely pure. You are light. Every breath now feels completely free and whole. Everything negative becomes light through your light.
Nothing negative can dim your light.

Take a deep breath, enjoy this certainty and now let your sacred ball of light become a small ball of light in your belly again. Your ball of light is now your companion and it will continue to glow within you and provide you with light. Take another deep breath in and out several times and slowly and gently open your eyes again, come back to the here and now and from now on be sure to be completely supplied. The universe means well with you. This is how it should be.

You feel a bit overfilled with emotions right now and would like to release them? Mother Earth will gladly accept them!

You can imagine a place or go to a natural place where you can stand with bare feet on Mother Earth. This can be the edge of a field, in the forest, by the lake, wherever you want.

Stand up straight with both legs firmly planted with bare feet on Mother Earth.

A ray of light will now flow like a gentle waterfall from above through your head, through your neck, your shoulder, your arms, your chest, your belly, your lap and your legs into your feet and from your feet directly into Mother Earth. Let all the things that you are currently clearing or can never clear take in Mother Earth. Mother Earth also takes care of you and accepts all that you give away. Let go and allow pure light to flow through you. If you feel something disturbing in your body, give it to the light flow and hand it over to Mother Earth. As soon as you feel better, come back to yourself, open your eyes, look around.

Where are you? What day is it today? What time of day? How old are you? Welcome to the now.

General basics

Finally, you need to internalize and understand one thing:

If you live in an environment that is unhealthy for yourself, you can try as much as you want to heal yourself with meditation, visualization or other methods. The first thing you need to do is to build a good foundation, and you create a good foundation with positive feelings about yourself and your environment, with good social bonds and with the feeling of being self-effective.

I can show you a thousand methods, techniques and possibilities, it will all be of no use if you don't have a good foundation. So get down to business and Holla die Waldfee, you will be thrilled with yourself when you learn things about yourself that you didn't even know, because you kept them hidden far back in the darkest corner of the closet that lies within you.

In order to be able to ensure a good basis for healing at all, access to a conscious diet is indispensable. In order to be able to master a change of diet in a meaningful and sustainable way, a complete emptying and detoxification is necessary.

FASTING

Fasting generally lowers your blood pressure, it has anti-inflammatory and pain-relieving effects and removes toxins from the body. I will introduce you to different forms of fasting. It is essential for a change of diet to first empty your body, let go of toxins and start again. Basically, as in the body, so in the mind.

Therapeutic fasting or water fasting: For about a week you eat nothing at all. You drink at least 3 liters of water every day. Please pay attention to your circulation, should you get great feelings of weakness, drink a broth or juice in between or change to another form of fasting. Allow your body some preparation time before and after the fast, for example by reducing your calories and general amount of food 3 days before the fast and start flushing your body already now. Do not work or do any other heavy physical or mental activities during the fasting week.

You should just focus on yourself.

This is now your process to yourself. You will get to know your own demons during the fasting week. In your head you will scream and this screaming wants to persuade you not to implement this new life. It wants to go back to the old familiar security. Once you have completed your 5 to 7 days of fasting, break the fast by eating a fresh apple for lunch and a fresh vegetable soup in the evening.

Buchinger fasting: Buchinger fasting extends over about 2 weeks. Here, too, it is important to be in good contact with your body and to support it with Glauber's salt to ¾ liter of water to be able to empty completely. Drink this mixture in 20 minutes and rinse with a liter of clear water. Within the next 2 to 3 hours, you will experience a typical diarrhea-like bowel evacuation. You can also use laxative tea or enemas.

In this fasting method you are allowed to take a small spoonful of honey. Also, you should always support your detoxification with binding mineral clay. In your build-up days you can do yourself good with psyllium or linseed.

Alkaline fasting: Typical acid-forming foods are avoided in alkaline fasting. Only alkaline foods are fed to the body, such as salads, vegetable dishes, fruit, sprouts, herbs.
Alkaline powders and alkaline baths will also help you.

Generally, you can also drink herbal tea and ginger water.

Intermittent fasting: This form of fasting is basically a lifestyle. You eat only in a certain time frame during the day, for example, 11 am to 6 pm. This way you give your body a daily night fast of 17 hours. Or you may decide to skip a few days each month or one day each week. By the way, animals do it this way in their natural state. They fast one day a week. They know originally and intuitively that it is healthy for them.

> **Note**: Avoid highly processed and animal foods and trans fatty acids found in hydrogenated fats.
>
> Drink at least 1, 5 liters of clear water every day, even without fasting.

GOOD NUTRITION - GIVE YOUR BODY WHAT IT REALLY NEEDS.

I'm not going to write here, eat this or that, because I'm not you and I have no idea about your body. And despite all this, I will keep my recommendations vegan, not because it's cool, but because it's time to get back to what's important. Why would we want to heal ourselves when the world is going to end tomorrow because our diets carry a lot of suffering. If you want to eat animal products, ask the hunter or buy milk from a farmer who does not torture animals for it. As a general rule, dairy products have a mucilaginous and rather inflammatory effect. The old misconception that you need cow's milk for calcium may have worked back then, but today we know that there are ingredients in nuts and seeds that are better tolerated by us.

Be aware that every action comes back to you a little bit, and if you are interested in the subject of self-healing, you should also be able to consider the big picture and not just yourself.

All that I can do in this book is to give you suggestions, ideas and incentives. And I can tell you that the journey to yourself is a beautiful one. It's like finally rediscovering an ancient best friend. And because this ancient best friend wants to stay by your side for a while:

Eat consciously, do things consciously, decide consciously what you support and why, for what purpose and whether it even makes sense now or you should rethink the whole thing. And start enjoying again! Eat once - one at a time - so you can find out how what affects you and your dear temple. And no, don't salt it. Get away from the thing that you have to re-salt every dish. Start tasting again!

Go beyond your habits and be open to new things. You'll be amazed at what's good for your body. How you can tell? You feel good, your skin looks fresh, you feel energetic and clear, your little inner voice says quietly and with relief "Finally".

Whereby I must note that when the body detoxifies, we do not feel full of vigor and good and clean, in this process can appear skin blemishes and physical ailments, but this passes when the detoxification process is over.

WHAT FOOD OUR BODY NEEDS EVERY DAY

It is our task to keep our body healthy and active. Therefore, you should also know what the basics are:

Our **brain** needs omega-3 fatty acids and good fats, so spinach, strawberries, avocados, flaxseeds, walnuts, apples, blueberries, red grapes, cranberries and others are important.

Our **eyes** need vitamin A, lutein, antioxidants and beta-carotenes and that is in broccoli, carrots, spinach, sweet potatoes, red peppers, pumpkin, berries, garlic, green leafy vegetables.

Our dear **heart** needs potassium, fiber, folic acid, alpha-carotene, which we find in bananas, broccoli, spinach, berries, oranges, tomatoes, carrots, green leafy vegetables, pumpkin seeds, peas, oats, sprouts, pomegranates.

Our **bones** need vitamin D, bromeliads, magnesium and calcium. Found in broccoli, pineapple, green leafy vegetables, arugula, almonds, mushrooms, cherries.

Our **skin, hair, nails** need vitamin A, C and E. So eat chard, pumpkin, cabbage, oranges, kiwi, yellow peppers, seeds and cucumbers from time to time.

Our **muscles** need proteins, chromium and omega-3 fatty acids. In sprouts, chia seeds, hemp seeds, green peppers and apples, among others, we find what our muscles need.

Our **teeth and gums** need vitamin A, C and D. If we eat mango, melon, papaya, broccoli, carrots, pumpkin and sun rays, we are well taken care of. Well, it's a funny thought how you want to eat sun rays now, but it's enough if you take a nice walk in the open air every day.

For your **liver** you may prepare beet, apples, artichokes, radishes and other fruits. I am sure you can already think of good recipes.

Her **bile** is below the liver and helps the liver digest fat. It needs a lot of water and fruits with a high water content and also olive oil, linseed oil and more.

If you eat kohlrabi, celery, nuts and berries now and then, as well as my favorite, broccoli, your **kidney will be** taken care of, because it needs vitamin B 6, D, E, and C.

Broccoli is an all-rounder, this vegetable has many great vitamins that we need. Now you may say that you don't like vegetables that much, or maybe you even say that you can't tolerate them, and I can tell you that the more often you feed your body with them, the better you will tolerate them. Our body weans itself off, but also gets used to it again. So we are changeable and in order for us to have a healthy foundation and a foundation to heal ourselves in the first place, a healthy life-style is essential. And if you have only read about it so far, start now! Piece by piece. Every day a little bit more.

GOOD MIND GAMES

Basically, everything you say and think is an affir-mation, that is, an idea. And if you think about it, you may notice that you often talk or think quite negatively in everyday life. This cannot bring good experiences. Let's rather take positive affirmations and create new worlds for ourselves. It won't help you to denounce what you don't like, because that won't change what you don't like. Rather, try to clearly put into words the desires you have. When you use an affirmation for the first time, it will not seem true to you. Would you have to use this affirmation if it were already true? See. Good ideas and mind games are like seeds that flourish in our soil. First they germinate, then they take root, then they sprout from the ground. As you can probably imagine by now, it takes time for them to become a fully developed plant. And so it is with affirmation as with self-healing. It takes patience.

Risk being different.

SO WHAT IS IMPORTANT TO KNOW?

Avoid stress: Our immune defenses are weakened by excessive stress. Stress hormones called cortisol and others are released by the body or a large amount of certain immune messengers circulate in the blood, both of which promote increased susceptibility to infections and cardiovascular diseases. If possible, avoid any stress, for example by taking small breaks that you regularly schedule and allow yourself. It also helps to relax if you realize that you don't have to carry the huge backpack alone, which probably still contains many things that you carry for others. Pass on. Let someone else do work that someone else can do, make your daily life easier. You are allowed to do this and you are allowed to be worthy of it. Be mindful of yourself and see what you can confidently cross out of your schedule. As you can see, there is no way around being in good contact with yourself. Suppressed negative feelings, fear, anger and sadness also cause stress if they have to be constantly suppressed.

Learn autogenic training, yoga, meditations, Qigong, Tai-Chi or progressive muscle relaxation. You are worth allowing yourself to relax in between because that is what has a positive effect on your immune system. When you practice yoga, meditations or qigong, you will realize that your breath is incredibly important. It will make you aware that our body breathes, but our breath can also get stuck; we get caught up in unpleasant thoughts or feelings. It is advisable to work against a stagnant breath, there are also various breathing techniques.

For example, try this one: You breathe in and out deeply 5 times, feeling your breath fill your chest and also more and more your belly. Be sure to breathe into your belly. Consciously notice how your abdominal wall rises and falls.

Next, for one inhale each, hold one nostril closed with the index finger on the respective side. Hold the inhaled air, switch sides, you now hold the index finger of the other hand on the nostril that just inhaled. Do this 5 times as well. How do you feel? If you notice that your environment could smell nicer, change this for your next time as well. There are excellent essential oils for this that you can also inhale. Make sure they are really pure essential oils. Treat yourself to something for yourself there as well: **only allow things into you that strengthen you.**

And look right now into your little head, what it thinks, because this is also an immune-stabiliz-ing or reducing fact. If you think bad things, you will feel bad - in the long run. Also, if from time to time you get into situations that are unpleasant, don't give too much power to the unpleasant.

Every time you get upset, you weaken your immune system, and the situation will still be the way it is.

Be grateful for all the challenges in your life and see how you can use an imagination to bring relief back to a situation that is unpleasant for you. It might look like this:

Mentally put yourself in a situation where you feel good. A walk in the forest, swimming in the lake. You know what you like, so hold on to it, conjure up a beautiful inner picture of it and call it your very own secret inner place of well-being.

Refrain from nicotine and alcohol. Both are poison for our body, they change cell and organ functions and thus promote cancer.

Laugh, and laugh cheerfully, at the top of your lungs. Maybe you buy a laughter yoga CD or you participate in laughter yoga groups, you will notice, it is a real pleasure. A hearty cheerful laugh strengthens the immune system, a fearful or shameful laugh does not. A cheerful laugh increases the activity of immune substances, a group of white blood cells.

Sing. Singing not only lifts your spirits, it also lowers your stress level. Cytokines (messenger substances) are activated, making the body's defenses fit to fight pathogens and tumor cells. Immune messengers that promote inflammation decrease during singing.

Get enough sleep. The body's defenses recover most effectively at night. Six to nine hours of sleep at night are protective, but too much sleep promotes depression. If you have problems falling asleep and staying asleep, make sure you practice good sleep hygiene. Make a clear decision to go to sleep now, put your cell phone away, turn it off. You may allow yourself to be unavailable while you sleep and just have time to yourself. Make yourself a favorite tea, open your window and let fresh air into your room for 15 minutes. Is your bed comfortable and pleasant? Do you like your bedding? Is it cozy and soft enough? Is your mattress suitable for you? Do you have enough space to sleep? If yes, then I still recommend you to listen to a CD with a sleep meditation. This will help you wind down and get shallow sleep, you may also like hypnosis. Try yourself. Your life is very special and not comparable with the life of your partner or the neighbor, you are allowed to have your own helpers, whether it is a sleep CD or a regular meeting at laughter yoga.

No one has to understand it, only you have to know what you like about it, and feeling healthier, more active and lighter is fantastic, isn't it?

Get moving. Why not take a nice walk in the nearby forest on a regular basis? We are not talking about over-exerting workouts, gyms or whatever. The simple walk is the healthiest thing we humans can do. Jogging, on the other hand, is very hard on the joints, infrequent but intense exercise also tends to have a negative effect, so why not just go to the forest regularly, take a deep breath and listen to the sounds of nature on a nice long walk? (Please remember where you came from to find your way back too).

Use the morning sun right away for your good mood. Let yourself be enchanted by your power, be grateful for this wonderful sight. It is best to always get up in the morning with a grateful thought. You can practice this. Just say some nice things to yourself every morning while you are still in bed. Just consciously arrive in this new day and welcome it. Our bodies need the UV-B component in sunlight to produce vitamin D. Not only for strong bones, but also for an intact immune system. Eat foods rich in vitamin D and spend time outdoors. You don't need to buy a vitamin D supplement as a matter of principle. This is not about becoming addicted to XY again, in which many supplements find their way into your house and you take vitamins in tablet form in the morning or something similar, this is about making a clear decision to live a healthy, active, joyful, and willing life that will keep your immune system stable. Basically, the first run of self-healing happens on its own, unnoticed and over and over again. We can be very grateful to our body for being so grandiose.

Treat your body to alternating showers or go to the cool lake. You can only bathe in the summer, but you don't have to. You can also do it in the cooler months and thus harden your body wonderfully. You will notice that you breathe differently because of the freshness, you may also do that consciously. How about taking ten deep breaths in and out, and then holding your breath once for as long as you can? And then off into the cold fresh. You will feel more alive than ever before. It is important to dry off quickly afterwards and dress sufficiently warmly.

On hot days, you should avoid cooling down with very cold water, it will only make you sweat more. Lukewarm water and Kneipp knee shower are better for us on such days.

You don't know the Kneipp knee cast? Here it is:

You lead a soft, cold water jet from the right little toe over the calf to a hand width above your knee, there you linger for five seconds and let the water jet travel along the inside of the lower leg to the foot. Do not forget about the other leg, otherwise it will be sad.

Dress so that you feel comfortable and protected. Your clothes should be warm enough, practical and of course you may like them. But stay away from belly tops in winter.

How much fluid do you consume? How much do you drink and what? Sparkling water makes your stomach environment a little more acidic compared to still water. Try to get used to it again slowly. You don't need this sparkling water. It's just latently addictive, that tingle in your stomach. But you and your body don't need it. Still water and tea are much healthier for us as a basic foundation. Why don't you drink half a liter of water first thing in the morning after you get up? This way your body is well supplied and replenished first thing in the morning. Juice does not directly count as a beverage. Juice belongs to the category of food. So with juice you can't well replenish your water balance, but you can put a shot of juice in your water to get some flavor in your water, or just squeeze a lemon in the morning and mix the juice with half a liter of water. Your body will be happy.

Balanced diet, high fiber diet with lots of fresh fruits and vegetables, seaweed and vegetable fats and whole grains are important. If you do not eat a balanced diet, you are missing a must-have for a healthy lifestyle, i.e. a basic tool for self-healing.

I will show you which nutrients are particularly important in the following list:

• Protein building blocks (amino acids): Nuts, legumes (such as beans, lentils, soybeans).

• Copper: nuts, whole grains, legumes, cocoa

• Folic acid: yeast, wheat germ, lentils, dark green leafy vegetables, parsley, garden cress, sunflower seeds, peanuts

• Iron: Legumes, oats

• Zinc: corn, legumes, whole grains

• Selenium: Nuts, asparagus, mushrooms, cabbage vegetables

• Beta-carotene (vitamin A precursor): Carrots, spinach, peppers, broccoli, cherries, grapefruit, sweet potato

• Vitamin B6: potatoes, nuts, avocado

• Vitamin C: acerola, rose hips, sea buckthorn, black currants, citrus fruits, cabbage, vegetables, parsley, wild garlic

• Vitamin E: nuts, vegetable oils, sweet potatoes

• Vitamin D: edible mushrooms

• Omega-3 fatty acids: algae and vegetable oils

Feel free to keep writing this list if you are missing something. You may. Use your curiosity to learn new things and discover yourself anew.

The journey together with me is now over. I hope I was able to give you a few helpful moments to take with you, which you can now use for yourself. One way or another, you have the full right to transform everything as you need it. And be clear, this is a journey that will last your lifetime. A friendly and loving connection to yourself, your body and your environment is not suddenly real through a thought, it is a steady process.

Glad you decided to have walked a bit with me. All the best and heal, heal blessings!